OLD TESTAMENT INTRODUCTION

Mary J. Evans

Contents

Copyright © 2002 Angus Hudson
Ltd/Tim Dowley & Peter Wyart
trading as Three's Company

Published in the U.K.
by Candle Books

ISBN 1 859854141

Distributed by STL,
PO Box 300, Carlisle.

Designed by Peter Wyart.

Worldwide co-edition organized and
produced by
Angus Hudson Ltd,
Concorde House,
Grenville Place, Mill Hill,
London NW7 3SA, England
Tel: +44 20 8959 3668
Fax: +44 20 8959 3678
e-mail: coed@angushudson.com

Printed in Singapore

Picture acknowledgements

Illustrations
Frank Baber: p. 21
Trevor Parkin: p. 8
Alan Parry: pp. 18, 24, 25
Richard Scott: pp. 3, 7, 11, 12, 14,
15, 20, 22, 23, 27

Maps
Hardlines

Photographs
Tim Dowley: pp. 5, 12, 13, 19, 30
Peter Wyart: pp. 28, 29

What is the Old Testament?

The Old Testament is a history of the nation of Israel. It tells the story of how this particular people was chosen by God, how they constantly rebelled against him and how they were rescued by him. It describes God's love for them, his patience with them and judgement upon them.

The Old Testament is also a library, a collection of thirty-nine different books. It brings together the writings of many different people using many different styles. It includes family stories – detailed accounts of births, marriages and deaths – and national history – victories, defeats, and tales of good and bad kings. It also includes poetry, law, sermons and dramas, as well as prophets' predictions, warnings and encouragement. *The Old Testament is also the handbook for Israel's religion.* It gives instructions for Israel's religious rites and celebrations, and sets out patterns of behaviour. It explains how to worship and describes what religious buildings should be like; it explains how religious taxes are to be paid and what gifts should be offered.

The Old Testament is also a collection of teachings about God. It describes what it means to belong to God – to be his people – and explains who God is and what he does. It shows how God can be worshipped and tells why he deserves worship.

The Old Testament is also communication. It is presented as God's own word to his people – dynamic, and potentially life-changing.

For many people the Old Testament is a closed book. The following pages give an outline of Old Testament history, a description of Old Testament

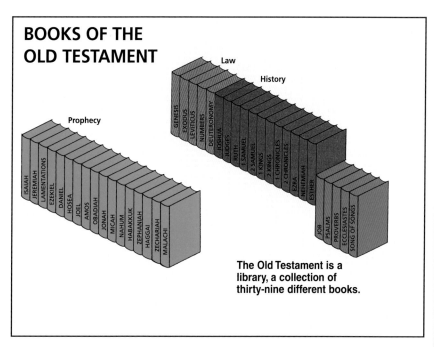

BOOKS OF THE OLD TESTAMENT

Prophecy: ISAIAH, JEREMIAH, LAMENTATIONS, EZEKIEL, DANIEL, HOSEA, JOEL, AMOS, OBADIAH, JONAH, MICAH, NAHUM, HABAKKUK, ZEPHANIAH, HAGGAI, ZECHARIAH, MALACHI

Law / History: GENESIS, EXODUS, LEVITICUS, NUMBERS, DEUTERONOMY, JOSHUA, JUDGES, RUTH, 1 SAMUEL, 2 SAMUEL, 1 KINGS, 2 KINGS, 1 CHRONICLES, 2 CHRONICLES, EZRA, NEHEMIAH, ESTHER

JOB, PSALMS, PROVERBS, ECCLESIASTES, SONG OF SONGS

The Old Testament is a library, a collection of thirty-nine different books.

literature, a summary of the main elements of Old Testament religion and an account of some Old Testament teachings. I have tried to provide a context in which the Old Testament can be better understood and appreciated.

The Old Testament was never intended to be a closed book; I hope you will be encouraged to open it.
Mary Evans, May 2001

A Chosen Family

Look at: *Genesis*

When we read the Old Testament, we quickly realise that history is story. The history of the people of Israel is the story of real people, in real situations, making real decisions, taking real actions and making real mistakes.

The preface
The first few pages of the Old Testament contain the history of the beginnings of the world, painted in broad brush-strokes. We learn that all people were created by God and were intended to live in ideal circumstances, sharing their everyday lives with God. But people were created able to make choices; they chose to go it alone and hence spoilt things.

The thirty-nine Old Testament books go on to tell how God picked a particular family – the Abraham clan – that grew into a particular nation – Israel. He chose them to be his special people, to show the world what would happen if people shared their lives with God. Sadly, on many occasions, this family and this nation spoilt their opportunities too.

But, as the story unfolds, we learn about God, his love for these people, his willingness to forgive and his great sense of justice. We get an idea of how things could have been if the people really had followed God's plans. A sense of hope kept them going.

Abraham's family
We learn initially about four generations of the chosen family. Abraham and Sarah, business people from the great city of Ur, in Mesopotamia, were called by God to leave their home and family and go to live in the land of Canaan. Much of the story revolves around the relationship of Abraham and his family with this God whom they were learning to know.

God promised them that the new land to which they were going would one day belong to their family, although at the outset they lived there as visitors; yet for many years Abraham and Sarah had no children. Eventually, when they were too old to have children, Isaac, the son God had promised, was born. Isaac's name means 'laughter,' and everybody seemed to love him.

Jacob the deceiver
Isaac's son, Jacob, was different; his name means 'usurper,' or perhaps 'deceiver,' and he lived up to his name. He deceived his brother, his father and his uncle in his attempts to get his own way. Later he had twelve sons and a daughter, by four different women, and made a favourite of Joseph, one of the boys. Although Jacob matured and learned more about God, his family behaved dysfunctionally.

Joseph's story
Eventually Joseph's brothers grew so jealous of him that they sold him as a slave to traders travelling to Egypt, but told their father that a wild animal had killed him. However, in Egypt, Joseph grew from a spoilt boy into a gifted leader. Although he was wrongfully jailed, even in prison he was respected. A chain of events led ultimately to his being given control over the Egyptian economy.

When, years later and in a great famine, Joseph's brothers came to Egypt to try to buy food, they had no idea that Joseph held their fate in his hands. Joseph's family were eventually reconciled with him, and he was able to see that God had used circumstances for good, even when some actions, such as those of his brothers, had been intended for bad. The whole family, including Jacob, finally went to live in Egypt.

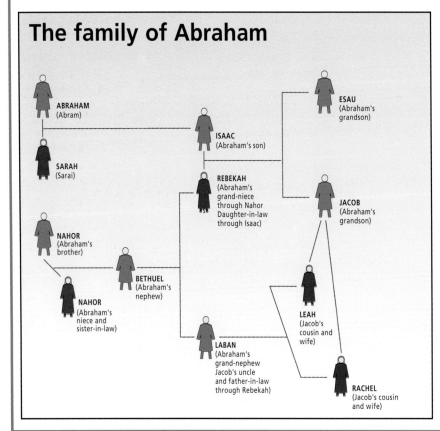

The family of Abraham

ABRAHAM (Abram)

SARAH (Sarai)

NAHOR (Abraham's brother)

NAHOR (Abraham's niece and sister-in-law)

BETHUEL (Abraham's nephew)

ISAAC (Abraham's son)

REBEKAH (Abraham's grand-niece through Nahor Daughter-in-law through Isaac)

LABAN (Abraham's grand-nephew Jacob's uncle and father-in-law through Rebekah)

ESAU (Abraham's grandson)

JACOB (Abraham's grandson)

LEAH (Jacob's cousin and wife)

RACHEL (Jacob's cousin and wife)

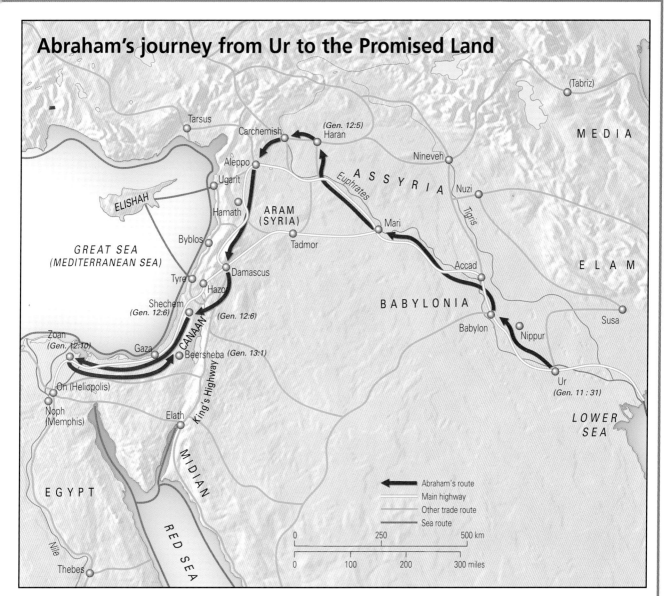

Abraham's journey from Ur to the Promised Land

(Tabriz)

M E D I A

Tarsus

Carchemish *(Gen. 12:5)* Haran

Nineveh

Aleppo

A S S Y R I A

Ugarit

Nuzi

ELISHAH

Euphrates

Tigris

E L A M

Hamath

ARAM (SYRIA)

Mari

GREAT SEA (MEDITERRANEAN SEA)

Byblos

Tadmor

Accad

Tyre

Damascus

B A B Y L O N I A

Hazor

Shechem *(Gen. 12:6)*

(Gen. 12:6)

CANAAN

Babylon

Nippur

Susa

Zoan *(Gen. 12:10)*

Gaza

Beersheba *(Gen. 13:1)*

King's Highway

Ur *(Gen. 11 : 31)*

On (Heliopolis)

LOWER SEA

Noph (Memphis)

Elath

MIDIAN

E G Y P T

Nile

RED SEA

Thebes

➤ Abraham's route
— Main highway
— Other trade route
— Sea route

0   250   500 km

0   100   200   300 miles

The Cave of Machpelah, Hebron, burial place of Abraham's family.

Reading between the lines

1. *God chose both parents of the promised son.* Abraham had other sons, but it was only the son of Abraham and Sarah who was to be father of the chosen people. Much is said about women and their interests; Sarah, Isaac's wife, Rebekah, and Jacob's two main wives all have important roles in the story.

2. *God chose Abraham and Sarah's family, but this did not mean he was uninterested in other people.* We also learn about God's care for Hagar, the Egyptian slave whom Abraham and Sarah treated badly, and his care for Abraham's nephew Lot, who made some bad decisions.

3. *The people God chose were not perfect;* they made many mistakes. But if they were willing to listen and learn there was always a way forward; God still wanted them to belong to him.

4. *God gave the chosen people the land of Canaan, but that did not mean he could look after them only there.* God was concerned with what was happening in the whole world, including Egypt, and his power was just as real in these other countries.

A New Nation

Look at: *Exodus, Numbers, Joshua and Judges*

For many years the Abraham clan lived as honoured guests of the Egyptians, since they were relatives of Joseph, who had saved Egypt from disaster. (In Egypt they became known as the people of Israel, the name that God gave Jacob). They prospered in Egypt, and did not return to Canaan.

However, after many years, when Joseph had been forgotten, the Egyptians grew jealous of this immigrant community. The Israelites became slaves, used ruthlessly by Pharaoh to construct his magnificent buildings. Eventually, more than three hundred years after Joseph's death, the Egyptians murdered a generation of Israelite boys at birth, to avoid any possible future rebellion. At this point God stepped in.

Moses saved from death

A determined mother, her daughter and a compassionate Egyptian princess were used by God to alter events. Israel was a male-dominated society, but women often played significant roles. These three women ensured that an Israelite baby boy, Moses, was saved from death, brought up in the palace and given an exclusive education. However, this made him rather arrogant, and if God was to use him, he needed to learn humility. Moses broke the Egyptian law, fled the country and spent forty years in an isolated desert community.

Moses saves his people

At the age of 80, Moses

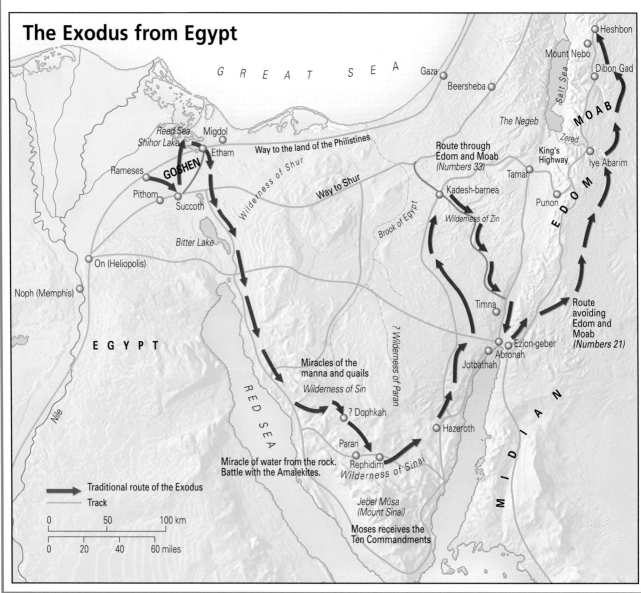

The Exodus from Egypt

GREAT SEA

Gaza

Beersheba

Heshbon

Mount Nebo

Dibon Gad

Salt Sea

The Negeb

Zered

MOAB

Reed Sea
Shihor Lake

Migdol

Etham

Way to the land of the Philistines

Route through Edom and Moab
(Numbers 33)

King's Highway

Iye Abarim

Rameses

GOSHEN

Wilderness of Shur

Way to Shur

Tamar

Kadesh-barnea

Pithom

Succoth

Wilderness of Zin

Punon

EDOM

Brook of Egypt

On (Heliopolis)

Bitter Lake

Noph (Memphis)

EGYPT

Timna

Route avoiding Edom and Moab
(Numbers 21)

Ezion-geber

Abronah

Jotbathah

? Wilderness of Paran

Miracles of the manna and quails
Wilderness of Sin

Nile

RED SEA

? Dophkah

Paran

Hazeroth

MIDIAN

Miracle of water from the rock.
Battle with the Amalekites.

Rephidim

Wilderness of Sinai

*Jebel Mûsa
(Mount Sinai)*

Moses receives the
Ten Commandments

→ Traditional route of the Exodus

— Track

0   50   100 km

0   20   40   60 miles

The thirteen judges of Israel

Othniel Caleb's nephew

Ehud a left-handed man who was a gifted strategist and killed the king of Moab

Shamgar

Deborah prophetess, skilled manager and gifted poet

Gideon a weak man, used by God to defeat the Midianites, but in his later years worshipped idols.

Tola

Jair

Jephthah

Ibzan

Elon

Abdon

Samson used his remarkable physical strength to good effect, but lacked moral fibre.

Moses and his brother Aaron tell Pharaoh to release the Israelites from Egypt.

reluctantly returned to Egypt, and eventually became one of Israel's greatest leaders. God used Moses to help his people escape slavery, through the Exodus from Egypt, and set up the legal and religious systems that were to provide the basis of their national life for centuries to come. It seemed that they were now ready to return to the promised land – and that Abraham's family could at last fulfil their destiny.

However, at the last moment the Israelites were too timid to go forward, and ended up wandering around the desert for another 40 years. By the time they entered the land of Canaan, led now by Moses' successor, Joshua, virtually all the adults who had left Egypt with Moses had died.

Into the promised land
The new nation was now in the promised land, but life was still not easy. Joshua was a good leader and achieved great successes, such as the defeat of the city strongholds of Jericho and Ai. The Israelites annexed large tracts of land throughout Canaan and re-committed themselves to serving God and living as his covenant people.

However, Joshua died before the new nation was fully established in its new land, and no national leader replaced him. The Israelites were not completely committed to serving God, and enemies within and outside the supposedly conquered territories posed major problems for them. The Israelite tribes were very conscious of their individual identity, but less confident about their allegiance to the nation, resulting in much inter-tribal conflict.

Highs and lows
The book of Judges records the highs and lows of these years, until the setting up of a monarchy eventually united the nation. The judges were regional rather than national leaders, and though they sometimes acted as legal advisers, they were normally military leaders.

The book of Judges is no collection of hero stories. Its narratives concern a varied group of men and women used by God to prevent Israel becoming absorbed by surrounding nations. The accounts make no attempt to hide the decline in standards since Moses and Joshua, or to justify the behaviour of the nation and its leaders.

Judges records, but does not praise, Jephthah's thoughtless vow, which led to the death of his daughter, and Samson's immoral lifestyle. Judges amounts to a sorry story of syncretism, disobedience and disloyalty, alongside a number of high points. In this book, the women come out slightly better than the men, and Deborah is the only major judge who did not fall from grace.

Reading between the lines

1. *God is sovereign*, but this does not remove human responsibility. A view of God's sovereignty which holds that nothing human beings do makes any difference is quite alien to Old Testament thought.

2. *God is righteous*; the people's disobedience and corruption does not alter that.

3. *God is in control* and can transform even apparently hopeless situations.

4. *God is patient* and does not easily give up.

5. *God starts from where people are* and leads them on from there.

6. *God uses all kinds of people*: gifted hot-heads such as Moses, well-meaning weaklings such as Gideon, wise counsellors such as Deborah and even uncouth louts such as Samson.

Kings to Lead

Where to look: *1 & 2 Samuel, 1 & 2 Kings, 1 & 2 Chronicles*

Samuel – prophet and judge – initiated the monarchy to maintain Israel's national identity and hold the country together. For about one hundred years the country functioned successfully as a united kingdom, but King Solomon's ruthless efficiency was detested by the northern tribes, and after his reign they broke away.

For the next two hundred years two kingdoms, Israel in the north and Judah in the south, co-existed. They were sometimes at war, sometimes in alliance; sometimes seeking to live as God's covenant people, more often turning away from God and ignoring the demands of the Law and the covenant. In 722 BC the northern capital, Samaria, fell to the Assyrians, Israel was exiled and the northern kingdom ceased to exist.

Beyond this outline, the story revolves around people, their inter-relationships and their relationship with God. We learn about the lives of ordinary people, particularly in accounts of the work of Elijah and Elisha and in the writings of the prophets Amos, Hosea and Micah. However, most of the records focus on the rulers and how they used and abused their power.

Samuel
Samuel can be seen as the last of the judges or the first genuine national leader since Joshua. He was a prophet, priest and kingmaker, who succeeded in holding the people together and making them think about God. He did not cling to power himself, but handed over authority, first to Saul and then to David.

Saul
Saul, the first king of Israel, was chosen and called, but not faithful. He was little different from the judges, except that his leadership was officially recognised and more permanent. But Saul became more interested in his kingly status than in the task God gave him; he began to assume that he could overrule God's commands – and was therefore replaced.

David
Although David never sought the crown during Saul's lifetime, when Saul died in battle he was pleased to take it. After initial skirmishes with Saul's son Ishbosheth, David took over the entire kingdom. Though a good soldier and diplomat, a committed believer and an able poet, he had a number of serious failings. He controlled the kingdom but did not always control himself or his own family, and experienced major problems with his sons.

Solomon
Solomon was in many ways the most gifted king of Israel. He inherited his father David's poetic skills, was a gifted scholar and brought prosperity to the nation. However, he led a life alien to the God's pattern of kingship in Israel. Deuteronomy 17 states that kings should avoid stock-piling wealth, dependence on military strength, idolatry, polygamy and oppressive rule; but Solomon's reign was characterised by all these.

Rehoboam
Solomon's son Rehoboam did not inherit his father's gifts, but followed his father's oppression of the people. It is not surprising that the northern tribes rejected his kingship.

The world at large
In addition to the regular feuding between northern Israel and southern Judah, Israel's relationships with surrounding nations were often strained.

In the north-west, Tyre (in modern Lebanon) was normally friendly towards Israel. In the north, Syria was growing more powerful, sometimes acting as an ally but more often as an enemy, devastating farms in border raids. East of Israel, Ammon, Moab and Edom caused the Jews problems, although after Solomon's reign they were weaker than Israel and Judah, and easily contained. To the south, Egypt was declining in

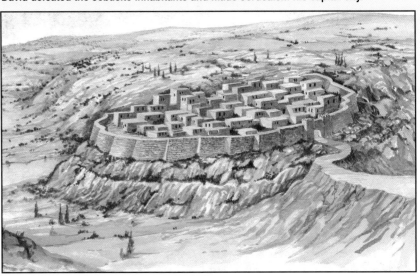
David defeated the Jebusite inhabitants and made Jerusalem his capital city.

> *But now your kingdom will not endure; the LORD has sought out a man after his own heart and appointed him leader of his people, because you have not kept the LORD's command.*
> 1 Samuel 13:14

power, while, Greece, to the west, was growing in influence: Homer was writing at this time, and the first Olympic Games took place at the time when the northern kingdom of Israel was disappearing. However Greek influence had not yet reached so far east.

Assyria, to the north-east, beyond Ammon and Syria, was emerging as the dominant power in the region. The Assyrian Empire initiated magnificent architectural schemes, but was famously cruel, with military power the key to status.

Israel and Judah were situated on important trade routes between Egypt and Assyria, and particularly in the late 9th and early 8th centuries BC, had great opportunities for economic growth. Assyria first dominated then destroyed Syria, and for a time Israel was left to her own devices. But this period of prosperity proved to be illusory, and Israel was in turn destroyed.

Israel: The northern kingdom
There were 19 kings of Israel, starting with Jeroboam. Although his reign began well, Jeroboam soon became more concerned to maintain power than to obey

Reading between the lines

1. *A good beginning is no guarantee of continuing faithfulness.*

2. *God will not give up on his people –* but those who completely reject the covenant will be allowed to live with the consequences of their decision.

3. *Economic prosperity and disaster were both used to make the nation recognise their need for God*; but the people had to respond in obedience and faith. Prosperity is not in itself evidence that God approves of the nation's behaviour.

God. In the books of Kings, all 19 kings are described as 'evil'; but these books were compiled in the south, and their assessments may not be unbiased.

Nevertheless, despite the ministry of such prophets as Elijah, Elisha, Amos and Hosea, and the existence of many true believers, Israel eventually ceased to be part of God's covenant people. 2 Kings 17 serves as an epitaph for the northern kingdom, making it clear that their demise was totally deserved.

Judah: The southern kingdom
During this same period there were 12 rulers in Judah – 11 kings and the notorious queen Athaliah, who killed her own grandchildren to retain her throne. Seven kings, six of whom reigned for 25 years or more, are described as 'doing what was right in the eyes of the Lord' – though this does not mean their reigns were perfect, as the writings of the prophets Micah and Isaiah make clear.

Corruption, injustice and idolatry does not seem to have been much less common than in Israel. However, the 'good' kings did make some attempt to lead the people within requirements of the covenant. Possibly this led God to be merciful to Judah, so that the kingdom lasted for a further hundred years before being conquered by Babylon.

The Kingdoms of Israel and Judah

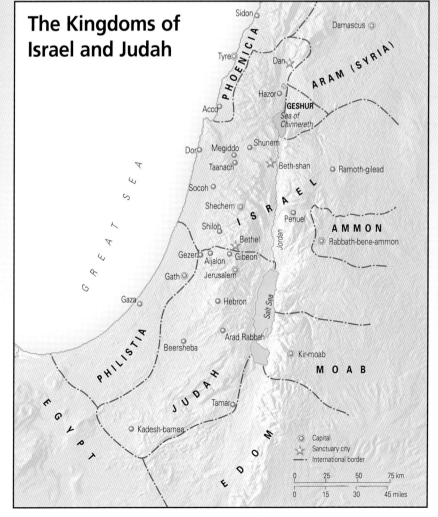

Exile and Return

Where to look: *2 Kings, 2 Chronicles, Jeremiah, Ezra and Nehemiah*

Hezekiah was king of Judah when Samaria was conquered and the northern kingdom fell. Influenced by the prophets Isaiah and Micah, and desiring to rule the nation of Judah in a godly way, he instituted a number of reforms.

Similarly, Hezekiah's great-grandson Josiah, who came to the throne as a small boy, also sought to reform both the system and nation as he grew up. These good kings and the contemporary prophets had some influence, along with a group of sincere worshippers, augmented by others from the north. (With the demise of the northern kingdom, the name 'Israel' is often used to refer to all that remained of the original united kingdom, that is Judah.)

The fall of Judah

However, the remaining kings of Judah ignored the lessons of the fall of Samaria, and allowed the desire for money, status, self-interest and avoidance of God's requirements to override the covenant and its demands. The political and military collapse of Judah can be explained as the combined result of powerful external enemies and internal rivalries. However, for the writers of the books of Kings and Chronicles, Judah's downfall was due to long-term religious and moral collapse, which Hezekiah's and Josiah's reforms scarcely affected.

Babylon had now conquered Assyria to become the dominant regional power. Babylon took over Judah, first as imperial power, allowing the national government to continue, but after rebellions, it besieged and destroyed Jerusalem and carried off much of the population into exile in Babylon. For Judah – unlike Israel – there was always hope beyond the destruction, even if for most of the exiled generation it was not yet in sight.

The Exile in Babylon

The exile started with key workers and students being taken to Babylon on a scheme probably considered to benefit a poorer subsidiary nation. Then, as Judah continued to trouble Babylon, a large group, including the prophet Ezekiel, was exiled in 597 BC, and a second large group followed after the destruction of Jerusalem in 587 BC.

However, life was not all bad for the exiles in Babylon. They could practise trade, plant crops, mingle with the local population and even work in the Babylonian civil service. They were also allowed to maintain their own community and follow their own religion.

Ezekiel spent his first years as a prophet in Babylon trying to convince the people – who still hoped to return to Jerusalem – that exile was a deserved punishment from God. Once Jerusalem had been destroyed and they had lost hope, Ezekiel's message changed to one of encouragement and hope for the future. The Jews' God was a God of grace, who would show mercy to a penitent people and one day bring them back to their own land.

Babylon falls

Then, in a remarkably quick turn-about, Babylon, was defeated by the Medo-Persians from the south. Persian influence rapidly

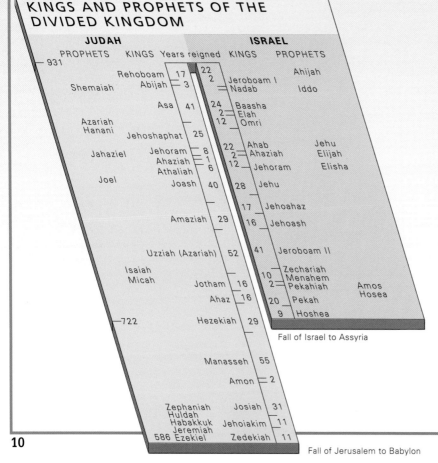

KINGS AND PROPHETS OF THE DIVIDED KINGDOM

JUDAH				ISRAEL	
PROPHETS	KINGS	Years reigned		KINGS	PROPHETS
931					
	Rehoboam	17	22		Ahijah
Shemaiah	Abijah	3	2	Jeroboam I	
				Nadab	Iddo
	Asa	41	24	Baasha	
			2	Elah	
Azariah			12	Omri	
Hanani	Jehoshaphat	25			
			22	Ahab	Jehu
Jahaziel	Jehoram	8	2	Ahaziah	Elijah
	Ahaziah	1	12	Jehoram	
	Athaliah	6			Elisha
Joel	Joash	40	28	Jehu	
			17	Jehoahaz	
	Amaziah	29	16	Jehoash	
			41	Jeroboam II	
	Uzziah (Azariah)	52			
Isaiah			10	Zechariah	
Micah			2	Menahem	
	Jotham	16		Pekahiah	Amos
	Ahaz	16	20	Pekah	Hosea
			9	Hoshea	
722	Hezekiah	29			

Fall of Israel to Assyria

	Manasseh	55	
	Amon	2	
Zephaniah			
Huldah	Josiah	31	
Habakkuk			
Jeremiah	Jehoiakim	11	
586 Ezekiel	Zedekiah	11	

Fall of Jerusalem to Babylon

The walls of Jerusalem were rebuilt under the leadership of Nehemiah.

stretched from Greece and Egypt in the west to India in the east, making it one of the world's most extensive empires.

The return

Almost immediately after coming to power in Babylon, the Persian ruler Cyrus instituted a policy of encouraging exiled communities to return home, taking with them their confiscated religious treasures and generous resettlement grants. Many of the exiles from Judah decided to remain in Babylon, but a committed group decided to return, and in 538 BC began to restore the nation.

Rebuilding the Temple

The returnees started well, rebuilding the altar in Jerusalem and laying foundations for the Temple; but the work was harder than they had expected. The land had been neglected, the people who had moved into the territory in the Jews' absence were hostile, and for several years harvests were poor. The Temple was eventually finished seventeen years later, after the people had been challenged by the prophets Haggai and Zechariah. Although the community survived, and sought to live as God's covenant people, it was weak both economically and spiritually.

Babylonian infantryman.

Rebuilding Jerusalem

Some sixty years later Ezra and Nehemiah, encouraged by later emperors, returned, giving the people new heart, and rebuilding the walls of Jerusalem. The capital city was restored, the economic system revived and religion renewed. It may not have been the triumphant return expected in Isaiah and elsewhere, but was nevertheless a remarkable achievement.

Sadly, fifth century BC Judah proved no better than her predecessors at taking advantage of new opportunities. Oppression of the poor and religious syncretism soon became rife. While religion became strong, it also became legalistic and introspective; ritual became more important than justice and mercy. It is perhaps not surprising that prophecy, which had formerly played such an important part in Israel's life, disappeared for four centuries – until John the Baptist emerged.

Glimmers of light

Old Testament history is seldom uplifting. However, through its pictures of human failure and disobedience we see glimmers of light. We read of faithful believers, and see a clear picture of the Creator God, who has made a covenant with his people: always there, always faithful, always just and with a plan that can bring human beings back into a relationship with himself.

The scene is set for the coming of Jesus. . . .

People of the Law

Look at: *Leviticus, Deuteronomy and Jeremiah*

The people of the Law

To Israel, the Law was not merely a list of rules that had to be kept; it was a gift from God to them, an agreed basis for national life and the means by which they could remain in relationship with God. The Law confirmed that God loved them, and that they were his own special people. In this sense, it brought them freedom – not a list of impossible requirements. We can begin to see why the Israelites were so enthusiastic about the Law, and such statements as 'Oh, how I love your law! I meditate on it all day long' (Psalm 119:97) make sense.

A Law for all seasons

Because God cared about the whole life of his people, the Law deals with every aspect of living. Rules about family and social life, treatment of neighbours, work, the army, food, justice, health and hygiene are combined with rules about national government and religious belief. Everything mattered to God: how you harvested your crops, who you married, how you treated your animals, which feasts you attended, how you looked after your servants and where you worshipped. All of these issues – and countless others – are related to the central question: What does it mean to be God's people?

The Law was not merely for lawyers. Of course there were special rules for judges, as there were for kings, employers, husbands, mothers and almost every other group. But the Law was a gift from God to the whole community, providing a means by which he could bless his people.

EGYPT

Sinai

The Ten Commandments

The Ten Commandments provide a summary of the Law. The rest of the Law expands on these rules, exploring what they mean in different situations. The covenant meant that the Israelites could relate to God, but it also affected their relationships with each other. Similarly, the Ten Commandments deal with relationships both with God and each other.

The commandments covered many areas, and the Jews applied them to almost every imaginable situation. While individual rules were important, it was still more important to have a 'feel' for the Law, a sense of what it meant to belong to God, in applying the general principles in a particular situation.

Jesus and the Law

In New Testament times the requirements of the Law were often summarised even more concisely as: love God and love your neighbour:

'On one occasion an expert in the law stood up to test Jesus. "Teacher," he asked, "what must I do to inherit eternal life?" "What is written in the Law?" he replied. "How do you read it?" He answered: "'Love the Lord your God with all your heart and with all your soul and with all your strength and with all your mind'; and, 'Love your neighbour as yourself.'" "You have answered correctly," Jesus replied. "Do this and you will live"' Luke 10:25-28.

St Catherine's Monastery, near Mount Sinai, Egypt.

THE TEN COMMANDMENTS

And God spoke all these words: I am the LORD your God, who brought you out of Egypt, out of the land of slavery. You shall have no other gods before me. You shall not make for yourself an idol in the form of anything in heaven above or on the earth beneath or in the waters below.

You shall not bow down to them or worship them; for I, the LORD your God, am a jealous God, punishing the children for the sin of the fathers to the third and fourth generation of those who hate me, but showing love to a thousand [generations] of those who love me and keep my commandments. You shall not misuse the name of the LORD your God, for the LORD will not hold anyone guiltless who misuses his name. Remember the Sabbath day by keeping it holy. Six days you shall labour and do all your work, but the seventh day is a Sabbath to the LORD your God. On it you shall not do any work, neither you, nor your son or daughter, nor your manservant or maidservant, nor your animals, nor the alien within your gates. For in six days the LORD made the heavens and the earth, the sea, and all that is in them, but he rested on the seventh day. Therefore the LORD blessed the Sabbath day and made it holy. Honour your father and your mother, so that you may live long in the land the LORD your God is giving you. You shall not murder. You shall not commit adultery. You shall not steal. You shall not give false testimony against your neighbour. You shall not covet your neighbour's house. You shall not covet your neighbour's wife, or his manservant or maidservant, his ox or donkey, or anything that belongs to your neighbour.

Exodus 20:1-17

'This is the covenant I will make with the house of Israel after that time,' declares the LORD. 'I will put my law in their minds and write it on their hearts. I will be their God, and they will be my people.' Jeremiah 31:33

The Methods of the Prophets

Look at: *Isaiah–Malachi*

One of the most important ways in which God spoke to Israel was through the prophets. These people – usually but not always men – had received a special calling from God. Some worked alone and some in groups, some were government officials and advisers of the king, others were critics of the government. Some were not concerned with government, but brought messages to ordinary people. Some spoke in very down-to-earth language, others used visions and obscure imagery.

Fortune-tellers?
We often think of prophets as those who told what was going to happen in the future – but that is not how the Old Testament prophets worked. In general the prophet's role was to help people understand what it meant to be the people of God in their particular circumstances. In many ways the prophets are better compared with business analysts than with fortune-tellers. Their messages were as varied as the circumstances in which their listeners found themselves, but the pattern is similar.

A variety of methods
Prophets could speak in parables and visions, judgement, salvation speeches, hymns, calls to battle, oracles of woe, triumphant proclamations and laments. However, although the prophets' methods varied, there were five main elements in their ministry:

1. Analysing the current situation. This could originate from thoughtful observation as well as from direct divine inspiration. The people needed to have a realistic picture of what was going on – and the prophet's role was 'to tell it as it was'. Often they denounced immorality, idolatry, injustice and oppression, while the people still regarded themselves as good and religious. In contrast, sometimes the people felt their position was so hopeless that the prophet's task was to help them to know the reality of God's sovereignty.

2. Telling the people how God viewed their situation. How did God regard their despair and disappointment? What did God think of their injustice and corruption? Did God share their joys? More often than not the people disobeyed God, rejecting his plans for them, and the prophets pronounced God's judgement on them.

3. Initiating change. The prophets wanted to change people's attitudes and behaviour. Having shown God's attitude towards a situation, the next step was to explain what God wanted the people to do about it: to

The non-writing Prophets

Fifteen prophets – sixteen if we count Daniel, who was more a statesman – left books, and their writings make up almost one-third of the Old Testament. However, these were not the only people God used to prophesy. Many other prophets are mentioned in the Old Testament historical writings, and they too were ordinary people with strengths and weaknesses, joys and sorrows.

Non-writing prophets included:

• **Nathan** who played a significant role in the life of King David. He explained to David what God thought about the building of a Temple in Jerusalem, and set out the possibilities for David's dynasty, if his descendants acted with integrity. Nathan challenged David with God's view of his adultery, and later intervened to ensure that David was succeeded by Solomon rather than another of his sons.

Elijah struggles with the priests of Baal.

• **Elijah** worked as a prophet in the northern kingdom of Israel for about fifty years, challenging paganism during Ahab's reign, proclaiming God's sovereignty over Baal and his prophets and encouraging those who continued to serve God in difficult times.

• **Elisha** succeeded Elijah, beginning as the latter's personal servant, but ending up influencing the life of Israel and surrounding nations. Elisha was one of the few prophets whose ministry involved events regarded as miraculous.

• **Huldah** is one of the few women prophets we hear of. When King Josiah discovered the book of the Law, as he was restoring the temple, he asked Huldah God's will in the matter. That it was a woman who was asked to pronounce on a matter of such significance was not apparently a problem for the officials or for the writer, who records the incident without comment.

Elijah's successor as prophet of Israel, Elisha was renowned for his miracle-working ministry.

repent, turn back to God, act against a particular enemy or let justice enter their lives. These and similar messages played a major part in the prophets' oracles.

4. Foretelling the future. If the people heeded the prophet's message and followed God's path, then the future would be wonderful. The Old Testament includes many pictures of a glorious future, when Israel, enjoying prosperity and hope, stands as a model to the nations. However, if the Jews failed to heed the prophet's words, the future would be bleak; the Old Testament also has many pictures of the disaster and devastation that awaited them.

The prophets referred to the future in order to influence behaviour in the present. Which of the possible futures lay ahead for Israel depended on how, and how far, they responded to the message of God sent through the prophets.

5. Telling the people what God was like. What was supremely important was God – and the people's relationship with him. God was real, God cared for them, they mattered to God. God would judge them – but he still loved them and they were his people.

The Message of the Prophets

Look at: *Isaiah–Malachi*

1. EIGHTH CENTURY BC

Amos and Hosea, the only writing prophets from the northern kingdom, worked at this time, as did Isaiah and Micah in the southern kingdom. Isaiah addresses three separate situations, which we will look at separately.

Amos

Situation: Great prosperity and great corruption in the northern kingdom.
Message: God's judgement on injustice must be taken seriously.

Hosea

Situation: Great prosperity and great corruption in the northern kingdom.
Message: God loves the people deeply and is hurt by their idolatry and corruption. Because he takes them seriously, they will be judged.

Isaiah 1–39

Situation: The country was prosperous, profiting from problems in surrounding countries and enemies being occupied elsewhere. A big gap had opened up between rich and poor, and the judicial system benefited the rich at the expense of the poor.
Message: God is great and will judge injustice and oppression.

Isaiah 40–55

Situation: The Exile is assumed to have happened, judgement has fallen and Israel can now look ahead to a new future.
Message: God is great and will save. This section includes some of the greatest proclamations about God's nature in the Old Testament, looking forward to the coming of the Servant of God, the Messiah.

Isaiah 56–66

Situation: This looks further ahead to the situation after the return from Exile, when the nation was re-established. But there was disappointment that hopes for the future had not worked out as the people expected.
Message: God is great, even when life does not appear to be so great.

Micah

Situation: Great prosperity and great corruption in the southern kingdom.
Message: God will judge the people for their injustice and immorality; but for those who repent there is a great future and hope.

2. UP TO THE EXILE

Four prophets – Nahum, Zephaniah, Habakkuk and Jeremiah – began work during the 7th century BC. The dating for Obadiah, Jonah and Joel is less clear.

Nahum

Situation: Cruelty and sin in Nineveh, Assyria's capital.
Message: Judgement upon Nineveh.

Zephaniah

Situation: Sin and irreligion in Judah.
Message: Repent while there is still time.

Habakkuk

Situation: Corruption in Judah

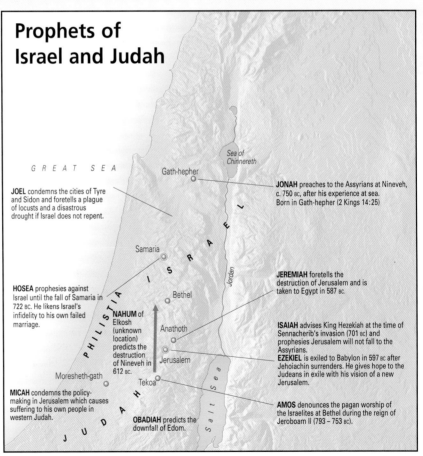

Prophets of Israel and Judah

GREAT SEA

Sea of Chinnereth

Gath-hepher

JOEL condemns the cities of Tyre and Sidon and foretells a plague of locusts and a disastrous drought if Israel does not repent.

JONAH preaches to the Assyrians at Nineveh, c. 750 BC, after his experience at sea. Born in Gath-hepher (2 Kings 14:25)

Samaria

HOSEA prophesies against Israel until the fall of Samaria in 722 BC. He likens Israel's infidelity to his own failed marriage.

NAHUM of Elkosh (unknown location) predicts the destruction of Nineveh in 612 BC.

Bethel

Anathoth

Jerusalem

Moresheth-gath

MICAH condemns the policy-making in Jerusalem which causes suffering to his own people in western Judah.

Tekoa

OBADIAH predicts the downfall of Edom.

JEREMIAH foretells the destruction of Jerusalem and is taken to Egypt in 587 BC.

ISAIAH advises King Hezekiah at the time of Sennacherib's invasion (701 BC) and prophesies Jerusalem will not fall to the Assyrians.
EZEKIEL is exiled to Babylon in 597 BC after Jehoiachin surrenders. He gives hope to the Judeans in exile with his vision of a new Jerusalem.

AMOS denounces the pagan worship of the Israelites at Bethel during the reign of Jeroboam II (793 – 753 BC).

ISRAEL

PHILISTIA

JUDAH

Jordan

Salt Sea

THE PROPHETS
and the kings who reigned during their lifetimes

		Kings and queens of Israel	Kings and queens of Judah
8th century B.C. 800-700	Amos	Jeroboam II, Zachariah, Shallum, Menaham	Uzziah
	Hosea	Jeroboam II, Zachariah, Shallum, Menaham, Pekahiah, Pekah, Hoshea	Uzziah, Jotham, Ahaz, Hezekiah
	Isaiah	Shallum, Menaham, Pekahiah, Pekah, Hoshea	Uzziah, Jotham, Ahaz, Hezekiah, Manasseh
	Micah	Pekahiah, Pekah, Hoshea *End of the northern kingdom*	Jotham, Ahaz, Hezekiah, Manasseh
7th century B.C. 700-600	Nahum		Josiah
	Zephaniah		Josiah
	Jeremiah		Josiah, Jehoahaz, Jehoiakim, Jehoiachin, Zedekiah
	Habakkuk		Josiah
	?Joel		
6th century B.C. 600-500	Daniel		Jehoiakim, Jehoiachin, Zedekiah
	Ezekiel		Jehoiachin, Zedekiah
	Zephaniah		Josiah
	Haggai		
	?Obadiah		
5th century B.C. 500-400	Malachi		

Message: God will act. Calamity follows disobedience and blessing, righteousness.

3. THE EXILE – AND BEYOND.

Ezekiel
Situation: In Babylon during the exile.
Message: Accept your punishment, love God and hope for the future.

Haggai
Situation: Returned from Exile, the Temple has not been rebuilt.
Message: Put God first if you are to prosper.

Zechariah
Situation: Back from exile; but where was the glory?
Message: Visions, and God's coming Day.

Daniel
Situation: In Babylon
Message: Stories of honour and resistance, dreams and visions of the future.

Malachi
Situation: The ongoing struggle in Judah. The people believed but were uncommitted.
Message: Get your act together! If you do, you will be over-whelmed by blessings; if you don't, you will be overwhelmed by judgement.

and her enemies.
Message: Amidst confusion and doubt, the reality of God remains.

Jeremiah
Situation: Babylon was attacking and Judah was about to be conquered.
Message: Be realistic about the situation. This is a well-deserved judgement from God, who will not intervene to save his people. Transform your lifestyle, accept punishment and wait in hope for God to bring salvation.

Obadiah
Situation: Trouble from enemies.
Message: Watch out, Edom! Israel's God is sovereign.

Jonah
Situation: Cruelty and sin in Nineveh, Assyria's capital city.
Message: Repent – or face destruction. God cares about the nations. Repentance is followed by mercy.

Joel
Situation: Life – and sin – continues.

I will raise up for them a prophet like you from among their brothers; I will put my words in his mouth, and he will tell them everything I command him. Deuteronomy 18:18

Poetry and Wisdom

Look at: *Job, Psalms, Proverbs, Ecclesiastes and Song of Solomon*

Poetry is not confined to one part of the Old Testament. Ceremonial poems and hymns are found in the historical books, while many of the prophets were also gifted poets, with songs and poems scattered throughout their writings. However poetic material is most heavily concentrated in the book of Psalms.

Psalms contains a unclassified collection of 150 poems, originally on five separate scrolls. They include collections of psalms written by individuals, notably David; collections linked to specific places; psalms of a particular type, such as marching songs, used on annual trips to Jerusalem for the great feasts; and psalms that defy classification. The psalms appear to have been collected over a number of years, in much the same way as a church hymn-book might be put together today. The result is a fascinating collection of songs for every season, occasion and mood.

It is interesting to consider the situations in which the psalms were originally composed and used. Note that the categories used opposite overlap, and that a few psalms do not fit neatly into any category

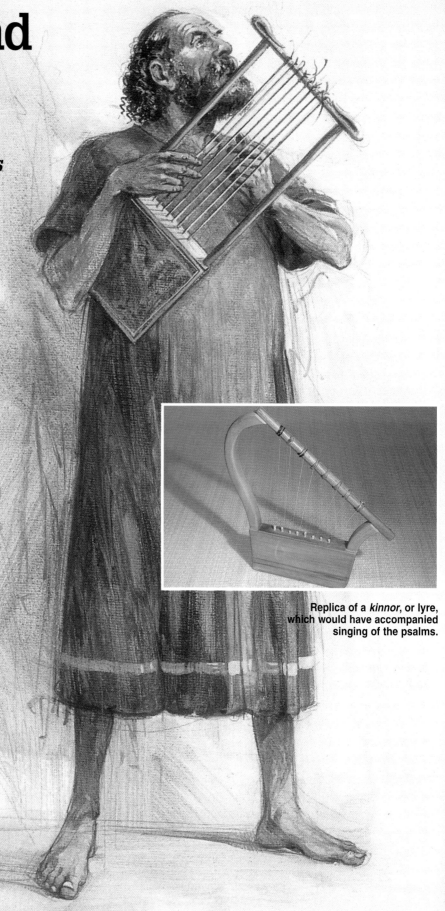

Replica of a *kinnor*, or lyre, which would have accompanied singing of the psalms.

1. Psalms of praise and thanksgiving

Some of these are clearly written for public worship and are intended to be sung by a congregation. Others are written in the light of some circumstance or incident, by or on behalf of a particular person or family.

Some psalms reflect on God and praise him for his majesty, compassion, justice or love, while others reflect on the wonder of creation and the created world. There are also harvest hymns, hymns for other festivals, and hymns recounting Israel's history and how God has constantly acted on the nation's behalf.
'*I will bless the Lord at all times. His praise will continually be in my mouth*' 34:1.

2. Psalms of lament or complaint

The Book of Psalms is often seen as the hymn-book of ancient Israel, yet although praise psalms form a large group, the largest group is of psalms of lament. Like the praise psalms, some relate to the whole community and were probably sung or recited when the people came together, while others are linked to individual circumstances. These psalms make it clear the writer is not happy – with his or her circumstances, his or her self, or often with God. They express, in vivid and emotive language, grief, confusion, misery and anger.

The psalmist may be persecuted, reflecting sadly on his or her own sin, depressed or simply perplexed. The lament psalms have in common a desire to express to God how the psalmist is feeling. There is no hint that the psalmists felt there were things too awful to talk about in God's presence.
'*Oh my God, I cry by day, but you do not answer; and by night, but find no rest*' 22:2.

The previous two categories overlap. Some psalms begin with despair and, as the writer thinks about God or comes into the Temple to meet fellow Israelites, gradually come to terms with it and introduce a note of hope. Others begin with hope and decline into despair. There was always a psalm that helped the Israelites express how they were feeling. Faith in Israel's God did not have to include pretence.
'*My heart is in anguish within me, the terrors of death have fallen upon me . . . . But I call upon God and the Lord will save me*' Ps 55:4, 16.

3. Other Psalms

Smaller groups of psalms include:

Royal psalms – written by a kind of national poet, celebrating such occasions as the enthronement of a new king or a royal marriage.

Teaching psalms – where lessons about faith and belief are expressed in poetic form.

Nationalistic psalms – to encourage the people in the face of danger from enemies.

Psalms of intercession – asking God's help for the nation or for individuals.

Philosophical psalms – reflecting on difficult questions, such as why the wicked prosper, and why the righteous suffer.

Jews visiting Jerusalem for the festivals would have this view from the Mount of Olives.

Religious Life

Look at: *Leviticus*

For the Israelites, worshipping God was not merely a matter of going to services three times a year, once a week or even more often. Although services and other religious practices were important, they symbolised that for Israel, being God's people involved the whole of life. For the Jews, there was no difference between 'religious' and 'non-religious' activities. If they treated people unfairly or disobeyed the commandments then religious observance counted for nothing.

Ways of worship

Worshipping God involved living one's life in the way that God had laid down. Family life, working life, social life and political life all had to be carried out in a way that honoured God and reflected his law. Regulations about

The young boy Samuel aids the High Priest Eli in the Temple at Shiloh.

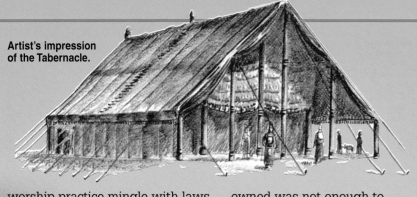

Artist's impression of the Tabernacle.

> I myself have selected your fellow Levites from among the Israelites as a gift to you, dedicated to the Lord to do the work at the Tent of Meeting.
> Numbers 18:6

worship practice mingle with laws about farming, fighting, clothing, commerce, loving and learning. All these areas were equally important in the people's relationship with God; all could be seen as part of worship.

But the occasions when people took part in specifically religious activities remained important. We look next at patterns of religious life in Israel.

The Levites

Israel was divided into twelve tribes, of which the tribe of Levi acted as assistants to the priests, looking after the religious aspects of national life. The Levites formed a kind of religious civil service, managing and administering religious activities.

In the early days, when Israel was still travelling in the desert, the Levites were responsible for the care of the meeting tent (Tabernacle), and for carrying the tent and Ark of the Covenant from place to place. Later, they were entrusted with cleaning the Temple and looking after the Temple furniture and implements. They also supervised the collection and distribution of gifts for the Temple and the poor.

The Levites did not have an area of the country assigned to them, as did the other tribes. Instead, they were allocated small sections of land throughout the country, so that they could help with local religious activities. The land that the Levites owned was not enough to support the whole tribe, so they also received payment from national funds raised by gifts and taxes upon the whole people.

The priests

The main spiritual leaders of Israel were the priests, who came from one clan of the Levi tribe. The priests were all descendants of Aaron, Moses' brother. Every boy born into a priestly family was prepared from childhood for a priest's work, but worked as a priest only between the age of thirty and fifty.

The priests had to lead worship within the Temple and administer sacrifices. When the people brought sacrifices to offer to God, the priests first had to ensure that they were properly prepared and then offer them. However, only a few priests worked in the Temple

High Priest in his ceremonial costume.

at any one time; the rest taught and gave advice. People who had recovered from infectious illnesses or skin diseases such as leprosy had to have their recovery confirmed by priests.

The High Priest

One priest was appointed High Priest. Once a year, on the Day of Atonement, he alone entered the Holiest Place in the innermost part of the Temple, where the Covenant Box was kept. The High Priest also worked alongside the king and the prophets in leading the nation.

The High Priest wore special clothes, including a gold breastplate inlaid with twelve precious stones, to symbolise the unity of the nation gathered to worship God.

Singers and servers

Musicians and singers, who took part in worship services, came from other tribes. Artists, woodworkers and needle-workers, who helped design and decorate the Meeting Tent and the Temple, also came from other tribes, as did those who served and helped when there were not enough Levites available.

The people

The servers, Levites and Priests did not however worship on behalf of the people, or excuse the people from their religious responsibilities. All the people – men, women and children – had an important part to play in Israel's religious life and should be counted among Israel's 'religious personnel'.

Religious Buildings

Look at: *Exodus, Leviticus, 1 Kings and 1 Chronicles*

Altars

From earliest times, altars were set up where people could worship God. They were usually simple piles of stones, set up to remind them of God's presence, or as a kind of table where sacrifices could be offered. Before the priestly system originated, apparently anyone could build his or her own altar; but later the system became regulated and worship was centralised.

In Israel, altars were made of stone, with no carving on them, and they were not usually cut to shape. This was to show that God was in control, and could not be manipulated by human artistry. Later, altars became more complex and were sometimes overlaid with metal. There were two main altars in the Tabernacle: just in front of the door of the tent stood the bronze-covered altar, where animals were sacrificed; inside the tent but in front of the Ark of the Covenant stood the smaller gold-covered altar where incense was offered.

The Tabernacle

After the Exodus from Egypt, the Israelites formalised regulations for public worship . Instructions were given for a meeting tent, usually called the Tabernacle, which would stand in the middle of the Israelite camp, to symbolise God's continual presence. This Tabernacle provided a focus for worship, where altars could be set up and the Ark of the Covenant housed. It was a simple structure, made to be dismantled easily and transported to a new place as the Israelites travelled through the wilderness.

The Tabernacle consisted of an inner tent made of brightly coloured, embroidered linen curtains, divided into two internally by a further curtain and hung over a wooden frame. The Ark of the Covenant was set behind the inner curtain. The tent was protected by an outer covering of goat's hair and a waterproof outer leather shell probably made from the hide of mammals.

This tent-like structure was surrounded by an outer courtyard, making the site about 46 metres by 23 metres overall. The site served not so much as a meeting hall as a nerve-centre for the community, where the people could come to present their needs to God and gather to hear God's word proclaimed.

The Temple

Once Israel entered Canaan and began to develop a settled lifestyle, more lasting worship structures were erected, such as that at Shiloh, where the prophet Samuel lived as a boy. Eventually, King David planned and Solomon erected a permanent Temple at Jerusalem. This was much larger than the Tabernacle, it was made of stone and included a courtyard surrounded by buildings.

The Temple court

However the pattern of the Temple remained the same as the Tabernacle: an outer court where the people could come, and a

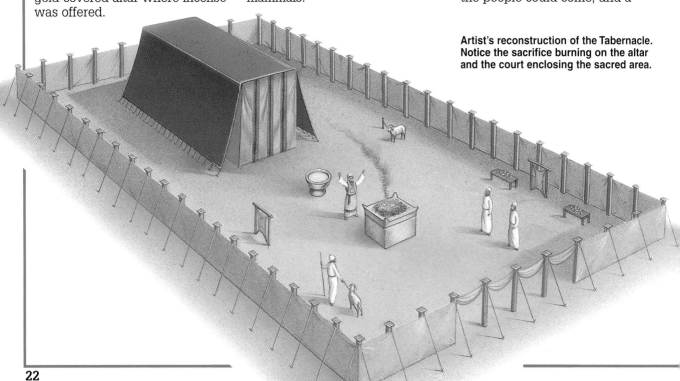

Artist's reconstruction of the Tabernacle. Notice the sacrifice burning on the altar and the court enclosing the sacred area.

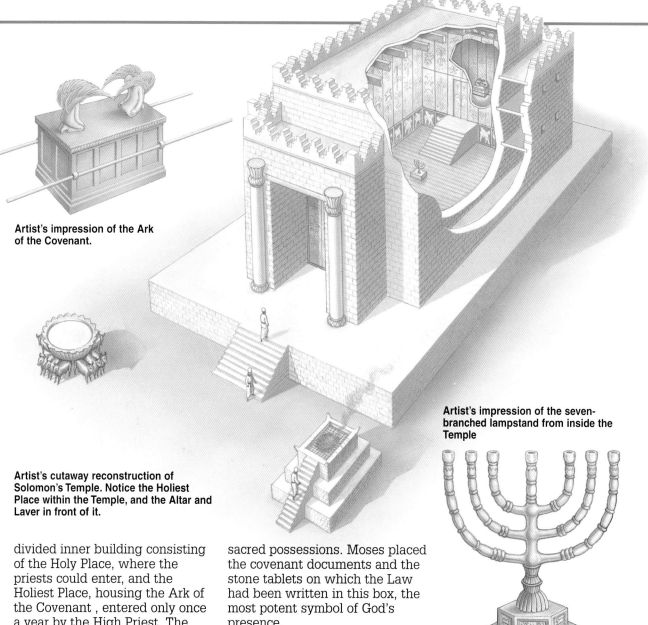

Artist's impression of the Ark of the Covenant.

Artist's cutaway reconstruction of Solomon's Temple. Notice the Holiest Place within the Temple, and the Altar and Laver in front of it.

Artist's impression of the seven-branched lampstand from inside the Temple

divided inner building consisting of the Holy Place, where the priests could enter, and the Holiest Place, housing the Ark of the Covenant , entered only once a year by the High Priest. The Temple courtyard was apparently big enough for large crowds of people to gather. Solomon's Temple was laid waste at the time of the exile to Babylon.

The returning exiles rebuilt the Temple, probably not as grandly as in Solomon's time, but to the same pattern. Several hundred years later, just before the time of Christ, Herod's Temple was built, rivalling Solomon's Temple in magnificence. New courtyards for women and for the Gentiles were introduced into Herod's Temple, but there is no mention of them in Solomon's Temple.

Ark of the Covenant
The Ark of the Covenant, or Ark of God, was one of Israel's most

sacred possessions. Moses placed the covenant documents and the stone tablets on which the Law had been written in this box, the most potent symbol of God's presence.

The High Priest Eli's horror when the Ark was captured by Israel's enemy, the Philistines, precipitated his death. But King David took care that the Ark was properly housed in Israel's capital when it was returned. Although it was understood that God was present and powerful everywhere, and did not live in the Temple, the intricately-carved gold lid of the Ark of the Covenant was pictured as God's throne.

Temple furnishings
A number of articles were used in Temple worship. Accessories needed for the altar included vessels to carry incense and grain offerings, knives for slaughtering

the animals and bowls for collecting blood. There was at least one large basin for the priests' use, for special washings, and probably others where the laity could wash. A large lampstand was kept constantly burning, and there were probably other lampstands too.

When the Babylonian king Nebuchadnezzar ransacked the Temple, he carried off pillars, the large bronze basin, pots, shovels, wick-trimmers, sprinkling bowls, censers and many other precious articles.

Religious Activity

Look at: *Leviticus*

Sacrifice

Today the idea of lambs, goats and bulls being killed and offered to God may seem repulsive, but it formed an important part of worship in Old Testament times. Animals were regarded as precious possessions, and it was costly to give them up.

In Old Testament times there were many different kinds of sacrifice. Some took place daily, reminding the people of God's constant involvement. Some were for special occasions, reminding them God was sovereign in all circumstances. Offerings could be of bread, grain or other kinds of produce, but most required an animal.

Three types of sacrifice
Special offerings were made at festival times, but there were three main types of sacrifice: gift offerings, cleansing offerings and fellowship offerings.
1. *Gift offerings* included burnt offerings or whole offerings, and accompanying cereal offerings. They provided a way for people to say 'thank-you' to God, and to show their love for him and commitment to serve him.
2. *Cleansing offerings*, known as sin offerings or guilt offerings, provided a means for people to show that they repented of disobeying God, allowing him to take away their sins and make them fit to worship him. The death of the animal symbolised God's forgiveness and the removal of their sin.
3. *Fellowship*, or *communion, offerings* were times of rejoicing and feasting. God was thought to be present at the feasts, and the people reflected on what it meant to be God's people.

In some sacrifices, the whole animal was burnt. More often, the beast was presented to God, killed by the priests before the great altar in the centre of the Temple court, cut up, and a portion of the sacrifice burnt symbolically. Often, the remainder was given to the priests as part of their wages.

The commonest sacrifice was the fellowship offering, where the priests received an unburnt part of the animal; the rest was cooked and eaten at the celebration feast.

Smaller offerings
The Law recognised that not everyone could afford big offerings; a gift of two small pigeons – something within everybody's means – was seen as just as pleasing to God as the extravagant sacrifices of the rich.

The Feasts

During the period of Israel's monarchy, three main annual festivals were supposed to be celebrated at the Temple in Jerusalem, though when the people turned away from God the festivals and the rest of their religion were neglected for years.

The Feast of Unleavened Bread and Passover
This festival took place in spring and celebrated Israel's escape from slavery in Egypt. There were also two more harvest festivals. Every Israelite male was supposed to come to Jerusalem three times a year for the important feasts. It was not compulsory for women to attend, because of the difficulties of travelling while pregnant and with small children; however they were welcome, and many women and children did attend.

Sacrifice at the altar before the Tabernacle.

THE JEWISH YEAR

The Jewish calendar was ordered both by the movements of the sun, moon, and stars, and also by the national festivals and the agricultural cycle.

The year was divided into months marked by the phases of the moon, with an extra month added every few years to adjust as necessary.

	Months			Months		Festivals
1	JANUARY	Winter		SHEBAT	11	
2	FEBRUARY			ADAR	12	**Purim**
3	MARCH	Spring		NISAN	1	**Passover and Unleavened Bread**
4	APRIL			IYYAR	2	
5	MAY			SIVAN	3	**Harvest/Weeks (Pentecost)**
6	JUNE	Summer		TAMMUZ	4	
7	JULY			AB	5	
8	AUGUST			ELUL	6	
9	SEPTEMBER			TISHRI	7	**Trumpets (New Year) Tabernacles/Shelters**
10	OCTOBER			MARCHESVAN	8	
11	NOVEMBER			KISLEV	9	**Lights (Temple dedication)**
12	DECEMBER	Winter		TEBETH	10	

The first harvest festival, at the end of the wheat harvest, is usually called the **Feast of Weeks**, because it fell seven weeks after Passover. The second harvest festival, which took place in the autumn, after the grape harvest, was called the **Feast of Booths**, or **Tabernacles** (both old words meaning tents). For seven days everyone lived in make-shift shelters, reminding them of the time the Israelites had spent wandering the wilderness.

The Day of Atonement (Yom Kippur), a few days before the Feast of Booths, was much more solemn. For this day the people, the priests and even the Temple had to be cleansed. The people fasted throughout the day, to express their repentance; animals were sacrificed and blood sprinkled inside the Holiest Place. (This was the one day in the year when the High Priest, and then only he, was allowed to enter this most sacred part of the Temple.) The ceremony also required the priests to send into the desert a goat, known as the 'scape-goat', to symbolise the carrying away of people's sins.

Sabbath

In addition to the major annual festivals in Jerusalem, the Jews marked the Sabbath every week. This was a day set aside, when no work took place, though it does not appear to have been a day set aside for worship services. Rather, it was a weekly holiday, to allow people to acknowledge God's provision for them and to give everyone, even slaves, a break from work.

The Sabbath was also used as a day for teaching, when parents would tell their children stories about Israel's history and what it meant for them to belong to God's special people. Children had to learn the Commandments, so that as adults they would be equipped to take their place in the community.

The synagogue

Later in Israel's history, priests and teachers gathered people together locally to give additional teaching. The Old Testament

A rabbi holds the Torah aloft in a synagogue.

does not mention the synagogue, but it seems as if this institution grew out of these teaching sessions, perhaps originating during the exile in Babylon, when it was impossible for people to travel to Jerusalem to worship.

Creation and Covenant

Creation

Where to look: *Genesis 1–3. Psalms, Isaiah 40–55 and Job 38–42*

It is taken for granted in the Old Testament that God exists – and that he created the world. Most of the writers' earliest thinking about God relates to the Exodus from Egypt or to the Covenant. Yet God's creative activity is a vital part of Old Testament teaching.

Two creation stories
There are two creation stories in Genesis 1–2, neither of them written in scientific terms, but both expressing truth.

Genesis 1 is a structured account of creation, which is totally God-centred. God sees, creates, says, divides, calls, blesses and makes. We learn that the world is ordered and purposeful; it is made the way that God intended – 'God saw that it was good'. The climax of this creation is humanity; human beings are created to relate to God and to each other, and to take responsibility for their own actions and the world around them.

God's work in creation is presented in Genesis 1 as finished, yet also continuing. God is the Lord of nature, who rules and maintains creation. He is not merely the initiator of life, but the one who sustains life, enabling the created world and the life it contains to continue.

The Garden of Eden
The Genesis 2 account is more human-centred. It does not recount the creation of the world, but the story of what happened in a garden in one part of God's creation. But the central teaching of both accounts is the same: the world is created by God and belongs to God; human beings relate to God and are responsible to God.

God the creator
Outside Genesis, when creation and God the creator are mentioned, the focus of thought usually includes:
- The intricacy and complexity of the creation
- The order and structure of creation
- The beauty and power of creation
- The purpose of creation: it involves God's will
- The uniqueness of the Creator
- The power and sovereignty of the Creator.

The consequences of creation
The Old Testament teaching about creation brings meaning to a world of meaninglessness. All life belongs to God; he has the right to make demands on human beings. They are accountable to him, and owe him awe and worship as their Creator. God, as the everlasting Creator, also has an ongoing responsibility to his creatures. He knows, understands, comforts, strengthens and enables his creation. He created the world and subdued chaos, and was also willing to subdue chaos in the lives of his people.

Problems in the world
Yet the Old Testament writers are also aware of the problems in the world. Creation as it exists today is not beautiful in every aspect; alongside it is an ugliness which is not solely the result of human mismanagement. The story of the Fall, found in Genesis 3, is only the first of many reflections on how it is possible to comprehend the glory and the dreadfulness of the created world as it is.

Covenant

Where to look: *Genesis 12–25, Exodus, Deuteronomy, 2 Samuel 7 and Jeremiah 31*

God created the whole world, but set up a covenant relationship solely with Israel. Covenants, or treaties – common within the Ancient Near East – were a kind of contract formalising an alliance between partners. They were not necessarily equal partnerships, but called for commitment and responsibility from both sides. The Old Testament develops this concept when it speaks of the relationship between God and his people as a covenant. Covenant is a very significant element of Old Testament teaching.

Contemporary treaties
The covenant between God and Israel is similar to contemporary treaties between imperial powers and vassal states. These so-called 'suzerainty' treaties followed a common pattern: they set out the history of the agreement, laid down rules the vassal must keep, formulated arrangements to keep the covenant document safe and to give periodic public readings, explained the benefits or protection that would be provided, and described the punishment for breaking the rules.

'I will be your God . . . '
In Israel, the covenant is established by God alone; he sets the terms. It is seen as a relationship between God and Israel. The so-called covenant formula 'You/they will be my people and I will be your/their God' is repeated in different forms many times, and lies at the heart of Israel's understanding of her life and faith.

However, the covenant was not forced upon Israel without her consent. She had the freedom to accept and confirm the relationship. The obligations of the covenant were not arbitrary; they summarised what it meant to be holy, and explained how Israel should behave if she were to enter this relationship with a holy God.

Now if you obey me fully and keep my covenant, then out of all nations you will be my treasured possession.
Exodus 19:5

Judgement
If human responsibility is taken seriously, judgement and punishment also become involved, guaranteeing the covenant, and opening up the possibility of repentance, forgiveness and restoration.

However, the setting aside of the covenant also remains a possibility. The commitment that God makes is unbreakable; yet the covenant ends the moment its obligations are broken. It is clear that, with Israel's constant disobedience and disloyalty, it was only God's grace and mercy that allowed the covenant to continue.

Five covenants are mentioned in the Old Testament.
1. *The Noachic covenant*, made between God and the whole creation. This was unconditional, with no human obligations; God committed himself never again to use a flood to destroy the earth.
2. *The Abrahamic covenant*, in which God makes promises to Abraham and his family. The obligations on Abraham and his family are not spelt out in detail, but they were called upon to remain in relationship with, and obedient to, God.
3. *The Mosaic*, or *Sinaitic, covenant*, the major covenant with Israel – so called because Moses acted as go-between when it was set up between God and Israel at Sinai.
4. *The Davidic covenant*, in which God made special promises to David about his descendants.
5. *The New Covenant*. Jeremiah and Ezekiel speak of a new relationship, in which God's law will be written on people's hearts and they will know and follow God.

Israel's God

If we see in the Old Testament nothing but Israel's sorry history, a collection of literature or a description of a religion, we have missed the point. At the heart of it is a picture of Israel's glorious God.

We learn about God primarily from the way in which he involves himself in the lives of human beings in real-time situations, not from theological sermons or doctrinal statements. Nevertheless, gathering together some of what we learn about him helps us understand why belonging to him, being part of his people, was seen as so special and desirable.

Four starting points:
1. *God exists.* This is taken for granted; it is assumed that only a fool would question it (Psalm 14:1).
2. *God allows himself to be known.* He wants people to know him, and reveals himself in many varied ways, through creation, through the law and the prophets, through visions and by acting in people's lives.
3. *God relates.* The purpose of God's self-revelation is not to give people an intellectual appreciation of who he is, but to allow them to relate to him.
4. *God is majestic and transcendent.* God makes himself known and, despite his greatness, he enters into relationship with human beings. Yet he is also unknowable; greater than any human being can conceive. The prohibition against depicting God in human or other form stems from this belief in God's transcendence (Deuteronomy 4:15-16).

The nature of God

- *He is living.* God is active not static; he reacts to people and to situations. He is Life, and no single picture of him could possibly be adequate. 'By this you shall know that among you is the living God' (Joshua 3:10).
- *He is personal.* The Old Testament knows nothing of the impersonal 'life-force' of ancient philosophy and modern science fiction. He is a living person; he has a will and gives himself a name. It matters to God what happens (Exodus 3:13-15).
- *He is spirit.* God is personal, but must not be limited by human ideas of personality. He is not a human being. 'For I am God, and not man – the Holy One among you' (Hosea 11:9).
- *He is eternal.* 'Before the mountains were brought forth or ever you had formed the earth and the world, from everlasting to everlasting you are God' (Psalm 90:2).
- *He is one.* God is a unity and God is unique. God is One and there is only one God. 'There is no one beside me; I am the Lord and there is no other' (Isaiah 45:6).
- *He is hidden.* Sometimes God is found at the point where he seems to be missing. 'Truly you are a God who hides himself, O God and Saviour of Israel' (Isaiah 45:15).
- *He is always present, always available.* God is not limited to the Temple, or even to the land of Israel, but is equally accessible in Egypt, Babylon or anywhere else.

The character of God

- *God is holy.* Holiness implies purity and apartness. It is a kind of awesome goodness that is simultaneously attractive and terrifying. 'Who is able to stand before this holy God?' (1 Samuel 6:20). God's holiness brings demands for his people. Because he is holy, they must also be holy (Leviticus 19:2).

And the glory of the LORD will be revealed, and all mankind together will see it.
Isaiah 40:5

SOME OLD TESTAMENT NAMES AND TITLES FOR GOD

Ancient of Days
(Aramaic *Attiq yomin*)
Daniel 7:9
The ultimate authority as judge of the world.

Creator *Isaiah 40:28*

Eternal God (Hebrew *El Olam*) *Genesis 21:33*

Father (Greek *Theos ho Pater*) *Malachi 2:10*

God of Mountains
(Hebrew *El Shaddai*)
Genesis 17:1; 49:25
God is all-powerful.

Most High (Hebrew *El Elyon*)
Genesis 14:18-20
God, the maker of heaven and earth.

God of all mankind
Jeremiah 32:27

God of the covenant
(Hebrew *El Berit*)
Judges 9:46
Maker and keeper of his covenants.

God of heaven
Nehemiah 2:4

God of Israel
(Hebrew *El Elohe-Yisra'el*)
Genesis 33:20

Holy One *Job 6:10*

Holy One of Israel
(Hebrew *Qedosh Yisra'el*)
Isaiah 1:4

I AM *Exodus 3:14*

Judge (Hebrew *Shapat*)
Genesis 18:25

King *Jeremiah 10:7*

Living God
Deuteronomy 5:26

Lord (Hebrew *Yahweh*)
Exodus 3:13-16

God of Armies
(Hebrew *Yahweh-seba'ot, Sabaoth*)
1 Samuel 1:11; 17:45
God is all-powerful.

Lord is my Banner
(Hebrew *Yahweh-nissi*)
Exodus 17:15
God gives us victories.

Lord is Peace
(Hebrew *Yahweh-shalom*)
Judges 6:24
God brings us inner harmony.

Lord is There
(Hebrew *Yahweh-shammah*)
Ezekiel 48:35
God will be with his people at the end of history.

Lord, Master (Hebrew *Adonai*) *Psalm 2:4*
God has authority.

Lord Provides
(Hebrew *Yahweh-jireh*)
Genesis 22:14

Lord Our Righteousness
(Hebrew *Yahweh-tsidkenu*) *Jeremiah 23:6*
By God's acts he declares and makes his people righteous.

Most High (Aramaic *Illaya*)
Daniel 7:18
God has final authority.

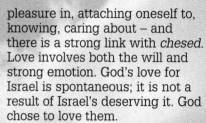

The Lord is the everlasting God, the Creator of the ends of the earth. . . . He gives strength to the weary and increases the power of the weak.
Isaiah 40:28-29

• *God is all-powerful.* His power is not arbitrary, but purposefully applied, working towards a goal. God is able to fulfil his goals.
• *God is righteous and just.* Righteousness, sometimes seen as an aspect of his holiness, includes – but is more than – doing what is ethically right. For humans, it involves conforming to a norm – to an accepted standard or ideal pattern. So it makes sense to talk about righteous weights and balances, or righteous behaviour, which conforms to the law. God's righteousness makes him concerned to see that justice is done.
• *God is faithful.* There is no adequate equivalent in English for the Hebrew word *chesed*, which is sometimes translated as loving-kindness or steadfast love, but also includes faithfulness, loyalty and total dependability. It is one of the commonest words used to describe God's attitude towards Israel.
• *God is love.* God's love for Israel is what makes the covenant more than a formal agreement. Many words are used for God's love, meaning desiring, taking pleasure in, attaching oneself to, knowing, caring about – and there is a strong link with *chesed*. Love involves both the will and strong emotion. God's love for Israel is spontaneous; it is not a result of Israel's deserving it. God chose to love them.
• *God is jealous.* God's jealousy is linked to his holiness and power – but also to his love. He is sovereign, and cannot share the love and worship of his people with other gods. The Hebrew word for this includes no sense of petulance or envy, so perhaps the term 'jealous' is misleading; 'zealous' might be a better translation.
• *God is angry.* God's jealousy may express itself in anger, which is linked with his holiness. It is different from human anger, and is never malicious or capricious. God is angry about evil. Unlike his love, his anger is momentary. 'His anger lasts only a moment, but his favour lasts a lifetime' (Psalm 30:5).
• *God is merciful and gracious.* This too is linked with *chesed* and with love. God's sovereignty means that he is free to give human beings more than they deserve, and he delights to do this. Mercy and forgiveness are pictured as freely available to those who, in repentance and faith, turn back to God. God cares about human beings and longs for their restoration. His mercy is never grudging.

God in Action

We cannot isolate the characteristics of God. God is not loving some days and just on others, merciful on some days and jealous on others. He is God, he is one; he is all that he is all the time. God cannot be summed up in a list of words.

We can profitably reflect on who God is, but we see him and know him mainly in what he does. Although we have many pictures of God and how he works, these can be only imperfect illustrations. We must take care not to assume that, because God presents himself in a particular way or doing a particular task, that this reveals all that he is, or all that he does.

God's work

From the beginning of the Old Testament, God is pictured as active. He does not sit back and watch what goes on, but is actively involved. His activity is varied, and described in many different ways; for instance God is described as warrior, water-carrier, healer, nurse, farmer and dressmaker. None of these *explains* God's activity, but all add to our understanding. However, some images are used frequently.

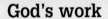

▪ *God creates.* He created the world (see page 26). He is creator of Israel, choosing a family and turning them into a nation. He is also creative in the lives of individuals. The prohibition against murder is derived from the conviction that all life belongs to God.

▪ *God redeems.* Many people today think first of creation when they think about God's work, but the Israelites were more likely to think first of redemption. They knew God as the one who had rescued and saved them. He had delivered them from Egypt and brought them into the promised land.

By providing the Law and the sacrificial system, God delivered them from the consequences of their disobedience and brought them into covenant relationship with himself. That is, he delivered them from being not his people and made them his people. He delivered them continually from enemies and disasters. For Israel, he was a God who delivered. Creation and redemption are often linked, particularly in Isaiah. God can use the world to work out his purposes in salvation, because it is his world (Isaiah 41:14-20).

▪ *God sustains.* He is the Lord of nature and the Lord of history, who rules and who maintains his work. Without God's active participation, neither Israel nor the world could stand. God looks after the world he has made and the people he has chosen.

- *God is shepherd.* This is one of the most well-known and best-loved pictures of God at work, and ties in with the picture of God as Saviour and Sustainer. God's shepherding of Israel is pictured as the working out of his *chesed* (see p. 29). He lovingly takes care of his people, as a shepherd takes care of his sheep (Psalm 23, Isaiah 40:11, Ezekiel 34).

- *God is judge.* Because God is holy, righteous and angry, he acts justly. God judges people now according to his just standards (Amos 7:7-9; Psalm 75:7); but there is also a future Day of Judgement (Amos 5:18; 8:9-10). The justice of God means that injustice must be judged, and the unjust will eventually be punished.

- *God is parent.* The picture of God as Father is well-known in the New Testament. In the Old Testament, God's parenting tends to refer to Israel as a whole rather than to individuals. He is Israel's Father, teaching the nation to walk, and bending down to feed them (Hosea 11:3-4) – which perhaps can be seen more as a motherly activity. (Similarly, Numbers 11:12 perhaps speaks of God giving birth to the nation.) The parenting images are intended to emphasise the love, care and involvement of God with his sometimes wayward child.

- *God is king.* For a long period of its history, Israel had its own kings. However, this did not alter the fact that their true King was God himself, who guided, protected and ruled the nation. The human king was always seen as God's anointed representative.

So, the God of the Old Testament is this great, glorious, loving, wise, creator God, who acts as shepherd, judge, redeemer and friend, and who relates to the people that he has chosen for himself.

He tends his flock like a shepherd:
He gathers the lambs in his arms . . .

Isaiah 40:11

Index

For Further Reading

General

W.S. LaSor et al.: Old Testament Survey (Eerdmans, 1992)

D.W. Baker and B.T. Arnold, The Face of Old Testament Studies: A Survey of Contemporary Approaches (Baker, 1999)

J. Bright, History of Israel (SCM, 1981)

R.B. Dillard and T. Longman, An Introduction to the Old Testament (Apollos, 1995)

W.J. Dumbrell, Covenant and Creation (Nelson, 1984)

—— , The Faith of Israel (Apollos, 1989)

P.D. Miller (ed.), Ancient Israelite Religion, (Fortress, 1987)

J. Rogerson, Beginning Old Testament Study, (SPCK, 1998)

Commentaries

There are a large number of commentaries on each book of the Old Testament. I recommend you start with those in the series The Bible Speaks Today published by IVP or The New International Biblical Commentary pubished by Hendrickson and Paternoster Press before going on to some of the books mentioned below.

Genesis – Deuteronomy

H. Blocher, In the Beginning (IVP, 1984)

B.S. Childs, Exodus (SCM, 1974)

P.C. Craigie, Deuteronomy (Eerdmans, 1976)

G. Wenham, Genesis 11-15, (Word, 1987)

—— , Genesis 16-50 (Word, 1994)

—— , Leviticus (Eerdmans, 1979)

Joshua – Esther

T.C. Butler, Joshua (Word, 1983)

S.J. DeVries, 1 Kings (Word, 1985)

R.P. Gordon, 1 & 2 Samuel (Paternoster, 1986)

T.R. Hobbs, 2 Kings (Word, 1985)

Poetic Literature

D.K. Berry, An Introduction to Wisdom and Poetry of the Old Testament (Broadman and Holman, 1995)

W. Brueggemann, Psalms and the Life of Faith (Fortress, 1995)

J. Day, Psalms (JSOT Press, 1993)

H.J. Kraus, The Theology of the Psalms (Augsburg, 1986)

The Prophets

W. Brueggemann, Texts that Linger, Words that Explode (Fortress, 2000)

M.J. Evans, Prophets of the Lord (Paternoster, 1992)

J.W. Miller, Meet the Prophets (Paulist Press, 1987)

A. Motyer, Isaiah (IVP, 1993)

J.A. Thompson, Jeremiah (Eerdmans, 1980)

C. Westermann, Prophetic Oracles of Salvation in the Old Testament (Westminster/John Knox Press 1991)